The Easiest

Financial

Formula For

The Widowed

By

Wendy Marshman

TABLE OF CONTENTS

Chapter 4
Investing for Your Future

Chapter 5
Planning for Retirement

Chapter 6
Estate Planning for Widows

Chapter 7
Debt Management

The conclusion

Introduction

The loss of a partner is often considered the toughest any person can undergo. The overwhelming distress you must go through can be intense and intolerable. Also, the chance of managing money independently can be intimidating as well for your own sake.

You will encounter various financial challenges like handling finances with one salary, analyzing your financial status, choosing wise investment options for the long term, and setting goals for your retirement. Also handling inheritance arrangements also. These economic issues may be complex and puzzling. Especially if you've never had to oversee your money earlier.

The positive aspect of this situation is that you and other women who have lost their spouses can adopt practical actions to regain the power of your money matters. People can organize for a stable financial future. The manual was created to aid you overcome the monetary difficulties that you might encounter. This offers useful tips and practical suggestions.

A key primary focus in this manual emphasizes the significance of adopting a proactive mindset regarding financial planning. You need to find time to comprehend your financial situation, govern your money wisely, allocate funds for the future, and organize for retirement. To gain a comprehensive understanding of your financial condition and execute the essential measures to safeguard your financial future.

This guidebook's main point is to tell you it's good to get help from finance pros. Working with money experts, tax wizards, or law folks can help you with tricky money and low spots. It also tells widows to learn about money stuff, making it easier to make smart money choices.

The big aim of this guidebook is to give you the right tools and help you need to feel safe about your money situation. By following the steps and pointers in this guidebook, you can make a solid money plan and have people around to help you deal with life's tough bits after loss.

Having a financial guidebook can assist in understanding your current financial status, future □ objectives, available resources, and effective management strategies for achieving those goals. It can also support you in making informed choices about□ investments, retirement, estate planning, and other long-term investment planning.

No matter the tough time you're having now, remember you're not alone. There's lots of help out there for you, and this guidebook is one of those helpers.

Chapter 1

Financial Independence

Embracing the journey from financial dependence to self-reliance is no less than stepping onto an open road, where each decision you make should reflect your unique goals, values, and circumstances. Financial independence won't happen overnight. It's a defined process, relying on a string of carefully made decisions, built on a sturdy foundation of financial literacy, strategic planning, and proactive actions.

This chapter aims to be your guide in embarking on this challenging yet fulfilling journey towards financial freedom, using simple explanatory terms that any layman can digest.

Key Components of Financial Independence

The cornerstone of any financial independence journey is financial literacy. It begins with grasping fundamental financial concepts, such as budgeting, the time value of money, compound interest, and risk diversification. As a widow, it is vital that you take the time to educate yourself - luckily in today's internet age, there are numerous free resources online, from eBooks to webinars, that can help you understand these concepts.

Next, you must devise a personal financial plan. The plan is the roadmap to your destination, displaying a clear path on how to get there. A sound financial plan will consider both your immediate expenses and your long-term goals, including funding for education, retirement or medical expenses.

Once you have a plan, it's time to start making smart decisions, reinforcing good habits, and putting your plan into action. This includes creating a healthy budget, reducing unnecessary expenses, and investing wisely.

The Nuts and Bolts of Becoming Self-reliant

Armed with a strong financial literacy background and a financial plan, you now have a base to work on the practical aspects of financial independence.

Firstly, analyze your current financial portfolio. Evaluate your ongoing expenditures, assets, and liabilities. Remember that understanding is key. If you're unclear about any aspect, seek professional guidance - this small expense may save you big in the future.

Your spending habits will have a significant effect on your journey towards financial independence. Cultivating frugality can help stretch your financial resources, while not completely sacrificing your comfort and happiness.

Another vital aspect of financial independence is learning how to invest wisely. Investment is not just about multiplying wealth, but also diversifying your income sources and ensuring financial security in the face of uncertainties. It's necessary to create an investment strategy based on your individual risk tolerance, financial goals, and time horizon.

Turning Journey into Triumph

The journey from dependence to self-reliance, while overwhelming at first, can ultimately lead to empowering victories. Along the way, the complexity of financial concepts will begin to unravel, and what once seemed baffling will become more comfortable with time and practice. The multiple investments that once seemed risky could evolve into your safety nets.

Coordinating a realistic budget can be a life-preserver, enabling you to stretch your income to cover your needs while allowing the flexibility to save and invest. It's important not to overlook small victories – even a simple act like paying off a credit card bill on time or allocating a certain percentage to a retirement account is a step forward on your journey to financial independence.

Remember, technology can be your ally. Numerous fintech solutions can help manage your finances better. Budgeting apps, online savings tools, and robo-advisors for investments can be a great assist in your journey.

And lastly, seek support when necessary. If the journey gets rocky, don't hesitate to consult with financial advisors or join support groups of people who are navigating similar paths. After all, connecting with others can add another layer of richness to your journey towards financial independence.

In conclusion, the path from dependence to self-reliance isn't a straight line, but rather a labyrinth where each twist and turn helps you become more adept at handling your financial future. This chapter aims to provide the foundational knowledge and practical tools to make that journey less daunting and more empowering. By the end of this journey, you will not only have achieved financial independence but will also gain the confidence and expertise to maintain and grow your financial portfolio.

Chapter 2

Evaluating Your Capital/Assets

After evaluating your current financial status, it's important to start thinking about the objectives you want to □ accomplish with your money in the future and determine the steps needed to attain them. Establish attainable goals that you can focus on ☐ and devise a plan to attain them. Make sure to monitor how you are progressing ☐ and modify your plan if required. Remember to review your plan often to make sure ☐ you are still moving towards your goals.

Assess your cash situation

This is a crucial step for ☐ widows dealing with spouse loss. As a widow, it is useful to assess your ☐ current income position when considering your financial status. To begin, gather together all ☐ of your financial papers. This means looking for things like bank statements, credit card bills, and□ any information about investments or retirement accounts you may have. Add up all the money that you haven't given back yet for stuff like houses, loans from people or banks or stores or whatever they□ are called, credit cards if you have them, and any other stuff where people gave it to you but they want it back now.

If you evaluate how much money you have, there might be□ areas where you can decrease spending and increase earnings. Learning about this will be crucial when you make a□ budget, set financial aims, and decide on an investment approach.

After organizing all the paperwork for your finances, make a note of the places □ where you get money and the things that it is spent on. This will give you a clear picture □ of your monthly cash flow. Ensure that everything related to how much money comes in is □ accounted for including sources such as receiving pension benefits. It's important not to overlook calculating recurring expenditures which can consist of either rental or mortgage charges associated □ with housing accommodation plus regular serviced utilities namely electric power consumption fees together with water supply costs.

You should keep tabs on vehicle loan repayments if they exist alongside monthly increments regarding☐ insurance apart from documenting routine purchases involving groceries or similar predictable costs incurred.

Knowing your income and spending is crucial for☐ widows who are planning their finances. This includes tracking your monthly income and expenses to☐ get a clear picture of your financial position. Start by figuring out all the different sources of money you have☐ coming in, such as social security benefits or any pensions.

Keep an eye on all the cash that leaves your pocket every month for things such as where you live (rent or mortgage), utilities☐ (water and electricity), food (groceries or eating out), moving around town (public transportation or gas for your car), plus any other regular spending. This will assist you in identifying the places where you can decrease☐ your spending or enhance your income to improve your financial status.

Identifying possible sources of income is another key☐ step for widows who plan their finances. This may include exploring job prospects, starting a small☐ business, or applying for government assistance programs. Remember to think about any other☐ possibilities for making money too. This could involve things like getting rental income from properties you own, earning☐ profits from investments, or discovering new methods of generating income passively. If you discover ways to get more money, you can create a☐ plan for using it wisely in the present and future.

Getting monetary security requires you☐ to set financial goals. It's challenging to determine where to allocate your money and ☐ evaluate your progress when you don't have clear goals. Breaking down financial goals involves categorizing them ☐ into short-term and long-term goals. If you can achieve something in less than a ☐ year, it is considered a short-term goal. For example, paying off your credit card ☐ or setting aside money for emergencies. Long-term goals are those that cannot be achieved quickly, but ☐ rather they require many years or even decades. Examples of long-term goals include preparing for ☐ retirement and owning a home.

Being specific and realistic is key☐ when setting your financial goals. An example of a short-term goal is having $1,000 saved up☐ for unexpected situations by the end of this year. A precise aim can be measured and executed, while a☐ realistic aim is achievable considering your existing financial condition. To establish financial objectives that are attainable and practical,☐ you can separate your objective into smaller stages. You can pick a deadline, stay updated on your achievements, and be flexible because aiming☐ for goals that are too tough can result in feeling annoyed and unmotivated. Make certain that the goals you set for yourself are☐ attainable and reasonable given your present financial state.

Reaching a significant financial objective is comparable☐ to conquering a gigantic mountain. Even though it may feel overwhelming, you can achieve it☐ by dividing it into smaller and easier steps. This is done by having☐ patience and dedication. Take things slowly but surely; each small progress☐ brings you closer to reaching new heights! Keep believing in yourself and your capabilities, knowing that by maintaining focus☐ and staying devoted, you can achieve your dreams. Don't feel demotivated, every individual effort you make towards your☐ aim is progress and brings you closer to reaching success! ☐

After assessing your budget, seek guidance from a financial advisor who will collaborate☐ with you to develop a budget that fits what's important to you. This budget is designed to help you stay within☐ your financial limits by controlling your expenses. In addition to this role of guiding investments or providing insurance advice a licensed professional such as a certified financial planner or investment adviser representative may counsel the consumer on strategies to maximize his or her Social☐ Security benefits scrutinize his or her pension plan analyze tax issues create an estate plan review existing strategies for retirement saving decide how much insurance to purchase suggest ways for individuals to get out of debt. As an example, your financial mentor could recommend that you switch over to a☐ more affordable phone plan or begin taking advantage of discount vouchers while shopping

When it comes to choosing where and how much money☐ to invest, a financial advisor is there for guidance. They help match up investment strategies with people's individual goals☐and comfort levels when it comes to taking risks. They know a lot about making portfolios that have a☐ mix of investments like stocks, bonds, and other things. A financial advisor is someone who can assist you in maneuvering through the intricate☐ investment field and making intelligent choices that correspond to your goals and beliefs. They can guide you in making plans for☐ taxes, retirement savings, and estate management.

Sadly, a few financial advisors☐ have dishonest intentions. Stay alert when working with professionals who receive commissions ☐ from selling stipends, investments, or insurance products. Instead, find a financial advisor who puts ☐ you first as their fiduciary responsibility. They will give you impartial ☐ and holistic advice. Choosing the incorrect individual to work with ☐ can lead to financial losses.

Financial advisors who get commission payments might try to sell you ☐ things that aren't necessarily the best choice for you. They could attempt to persuade you to invest in products that produce the ☐ highest earnings, without considering if they are truly right for you. If you choose a fiduciary financial advisor, they□ must legally put your needs first. They will provide unbiased guidance and aid□ you in making educated choices.

Regularly review and update□ your cash budget. Your aims might differ when your economic condition differs, □ and it's essential to adapt them accurately. When you take these actions, it makes certain that you are continuously working□ towards achieving your monetary targets and having a secure and cozy existence. Let's say you get a□ surprise bonus at work. You can think about changing your cash goal to save the bonus□ for something fun like buying a car or going on vacation.

One thing you can do is create a□ budget and monitor your spending habits. If there is a financial guidebook at hand, it can□ aid in identifying and ranking your financial goals. Consequently, this will allow you to create□ an action plan for attaining them. Moreover, it can support you in researching and comprehending different financial products and services,□ empowering you to make educated choices about your investments, retirement, and estate planning.

In addition, a monetary guidebook can furnish you with tips on how to optimally control☐ and safeguard your finances, so that you can reach your monetary aspirations sooner. By doing these actions, you can protect your money and build☐ a stronger future for yourself and those dear to you. Nevertheless, there could be some folks who don't think a financial guidebook is☐ needed, especially if they are already comfortable with handling their money well.

When it comes to choosing where and how much money☐ to invest, a financial advisor is there for guidance. They help match up investment strategies with people's individual goals☐and comfort levels when it comes to taking risks. They know a lot about making portfolios that have a☐ mix of investments like stocks, bonds, and other things. A financial advisor is someone who can assist you in maneuvering through the intricate☐ investment field and making intelligent choices that correspond to your goals and beliefs. They can guide you in making plans for☐ taxes, retirement savings, and estate management.

Regularly review and update☐ your cash budget. Your aims might differ when your economic condition differs, □ and it's essential to adapt them accurately. When you take these actions, it makes certain that you are continuously working □ towards achieving your monetary targets and having a secure and cozy existence. Let's say you get a □ surprise bonus at work. You can think about changing your cash goal to save the bonus □ for something fun like buying a car or going on vacation.

Having a financial guidebook can assist in understanding your current financial status, future □ objectives, available resources, and effective management strategies for achieving those goals. It can also support you in making informed choices about☐ investments, retirement, estate planning, and other long-term investment planning. One thing you can do is create a☐ budget and monitor your spending habits. If there is a financial guidebook at hand, it can☐ aid in identifying and ranking your financial goals.

Consequently, this will allow you to create☐an action plan for attaining them. Moreover, it can support you in researching and comprehending different financial products and services,☐empowering you to make educated choices about your investments, retirement, and estate planning. In addition, a monetary guidebook can furnish you with tips on how to optimally control□ and safeguard your finances, so that you can reach your monetary aspirations sooner.

By doing these actions, you can protect your money and build□ a stronger future for yourself and those dear to you. Nevertheless, there could be some folks who don't think a financial guidebook is□ needed, especially if they are already comfortable with handling their money well. Furthermore, certain individuals may feel that they can acquire all the required□ information from digital platforms or by consulting a financial advisor.

Chapter 3

Managing Your Finances

After examining your financial situation, the next thing☐ to do is effectively manage your money. Dealing with your finances can be difficult after becoming a widow, particularly☐ if you were not involved in managing the family's money previously. This includes creating a budget, tracking your spending, ☐ and finding ways to reduce your expenses.

Creating a budget ☐

It means creating a budget to decide how☐ you will use your money every month.

To start, jot down all the different☐ sources where you get money from. After compiling a comprehensive record of both what you earn and what you spend, it's☐ time to establish a budget that balances out your income with your expenses. If you take these steps, it will stop any wastage of money and guarantee☐ that there is enough cash to cover your bills and other necessary items.

Tracking your spending

This is another significant element☐ of controlling your funds. It's important to remember and record☐ all the money you use. This includes buying groceries, filling up your car☐ with gas, and any other expenses. Tracking your spending can be done using various tools such☐ as a basic spreadsheet or a planning app.

If you monitor your expenses closely, it will enable you to identify areas□ where excessive spending is happening and brainstorm ways to reduce it. You might realize that you're using up a lot of money on dining out or unnecessary subscriptions,□ and you can modify your budget appropriately to decrease those expenditures.

Reducing your bills

Cutting down on expenses can help□ you improve your money situation. If you limit your spending on unnecessary items, there will be□ more funds left for savings or other financial aspirations. Here are some practical ways☐ to lower your expenses:

i). Cut back on non-compulsory expenses

Look for areas where you can cut☐ back on discretionary costs,
 such as eating out, entertainment, or shopping. While you don't need to completely remove these expenses, ☐reducing them can alter your entire budget.

ii). Shop around for better deals

If you have regular expenses such as insurance fees, utility bills, ☐and phone charges, it is worth exploring different options to find the most affordable ones. It's possible that you can save money by☐ changing providers or discussing better rates. ☐

iii). Avoid impulse purchases

Impulse purchases are when we buy☐ things without planning because we suddenly want them. Even if you didn't plan on it, sometimes you might☐ make a big purchase like getting a new TV. Though you might think buying these items is harmless at☐ the moment, it can quickly derail your budget.

To prevent impulse purchases, you can stop and think about whether☐ it's something you actually need or just a temporary desire. Ponder if you would still want or need the□ item in a week or a month. If the response is negative, then it's□ unlikely to be a worthwhile purchase. □

By preparing a shopping list beforehand and strictly adhering to□ it, you can stay away from impulse purchases. This will help you stay focused on what you need□ and avoid the urge to buy things you don't.

iv). Use coupons and□ reserve funds

Explore deals and boundaries on□ items you consistently get. You can look for coupons and arrangements past the☐ week after week round via the post office. Consider utilizing applications like Ibotta and Flipp to track down☐ producer advancements and direct refunds from partaking retailers. Also, many stores offer saving projects and applications that can☐ assist you with tracking down arrangements and limits. You can likewise find coupons and limits via online entertainment, for example, a business'☐ Facebook page however it's critical to ensure they are genuine and not tricks. This can assist you with getting a good☐deal on food, clothing, and different essentials.

v). Decreasing energy utilization

Switching out lights and turning off hardware when not being used can greatly reduce your month-to-month☐ service charges, which can assist you with setting aside more cash after some time. Also, adding protection, utilizing energy-effective apparatuses, and fixing air holes can☐ additionally reduce your energy utilization and expenses in your home.

vi). Cutting back your home or moving to a more affordable place

This can likewise be a brilliant monetary move, particularly for the bereft who are resigned or approaching retirement. By cutting back your home, you can lessen your home loan installments, local charges, and upkeep costs. Moving to a more reasonable region can likewise assist you with getting a good deal on lodging bills, as well as different expenses of living, like food and transportation. Notwithstanding, it is essential to gauge the psychological and monetary expenses of moving, as well as to consider stowed-away expenses, for example, mortgage holders' affiliation charges and showcasing costs.

By decreasing your expenses and being aware of your ways of

managing money, you can free up more money to put towards savings or other financial goals. This can assist you with accomplishing monetary security and pave the way for a better future.

Chapter 4

Investing for Your Future

Investing for the future as a widow is an important step in securing the stability and independence of your finances. This involves making smart decisions that would take your finances to greater heights thereby increasing your wealth over time Here are some tips and strategies to consider when investing for your future as a widow:

Seek Help From a Finance Expert

Seeking to work with the advice and guidance of a financial guru in managing your capital as a widow will go a long way in boosting your economic stability. They would first take a thorough look at your whole economic situation and show you the best way and also help you choose the best plan that is just right to make your business soar.

They will also give you a helping hand on how to spend less funds, pay off debts (in case you have any), and save more money than before.

These money experts can help you make vital decisions since they know a lot about managing money and give you the best advice that will enable you to understand complicated money matters and make smart choices too. For instance, the advice of a finance expert can also help you with other important money stuff like giving you ideas on how to invest your money wisely, helping you plan for taxes, retirement, and what happens to your money after you pass away. They can make sure you follow all the rules and help you make the most of your money.

Choosing Safer Investments

It's very crucial to handle your money wisely as a widow. By choosing less risky investments, you can avoid losing the money you've worked hard for. Let's examine a few possibilities that can help cushion these risks:

i). Bonds

A great option is to allocate your money to bonds. It's equivalent to extending a loan to a company or the government.; they will guarantee that they will give you back the borrowed amount of money and provide an additional amount called interest. It's like when you loan some money to your buddy and they repay you with a small bonus as an act of gratitude.

ii). Mutual funds

Mutual funds or ETFs are another possible investment choice you can consider. These are like a fusion of various investments. It's comparable to having a bin with various sorts of fruits. Even if one fruit becomes rotten, you still have other fruits to savor!

Remember to keep your money safe, it is vital to be alert and up-to-date always in monitoring your investments to avoid risks that would hurt your business. Make wise decisions with your money and select investments that safeguard your future.

iii).   Exchange-traded funds(ETFs)

Exchange-traded funds(ETFs) which are just like mutual funds will allow you to pool money from various investors and invest in different types of assets. ETFs have a unique feature: they can be bought and sold on an exchange, making it as simple as trading stocks.

The reason why ETFs are seen as low-risk is because they allocate your money among multiple investments. For you as a widow, this provides convenience in managing and modifying your investments. Always remember that there are risks associated with every investment, so it's vital to do thorough research and seek guidance from a finance specialist before making any substantial decisions.

Chapter 5

Planning For Retirement

It can be especially challenging to pass through the world of finance and investment planning strategy as a widow. However, with the right resources and guidance, it is possible to take control of your financial future and security.

Ultimately, the key to achieving monetary security as a widow is taking a proactive approach to financial planning and seeking the guidance of trusted professionals. By developing a solid understanding of investing, creating a strategic investment plan, and managing risk effectively, widows can achieve financial peace of mind and secure their financial future.

Managing risk is also a critical component of any investment. While all investments carry some level of risk, it's important to understand how to minimize this risk through careful planning and research.

When planning for your retirement as a widow, financial planning is an important aspect that cannot be over-emphasized. It's essential to understand the different types of retirement benefits available and develop a strategy for saving for retirement to ensure financial security in the later years.

Pension

One of the most significant retirement benefits is a pension, which is a retirement plan provided by an employer. A pension is like a salary that you get after you retire. You get to be paid out monthly or annually. Pensions can provide a steady stream of income in retirement, but they can also be complex and difficult to understand.

Pensions can be either defined benefits or defined contribution plans. Defined benefit plans promise to pay a certain amount of money to retirees, regardless of how much money they have saved. These plans are becoming increasingly rare, as employers are moving away from them. Defined contribution plans require employees to contribute a certain amount of money to their retirement savings each year.

The money in these plans is invested, and the amount of money retirees receive in retirement depends on how well the investments perform. Widows should take the time to understand their pension benefits, including the vesting schedule, payout options, and survivor benefits.

Social Security Benefits

Social Security benefits are another important source of retirement income. It is a government program that provides retirement benefits to eligible workers. The amount of Social Security benefits you receive depends on your earnings history and the age at which you retire. Widows may be eligible for survivor benefits based on their spouse's Social Security earnings record. It's essential to understand the eligibility requirements and the impact of claiming benefits at different ages.

Strategies for Saving for Retirement

There are several strategies you can use to save for retirement. Some of the most common strategies include:

i). Contribute to your employer's 401(k) plan

A 401(k) plan is a retirement savings plan that is offered by employers. Employees can contribute a portion of their salary to their 401(k) plan, and the money is invested. Many employers offer matching contributions, which means they will contribute money to your 401(k) plan for every dollar you contribute.

ii). Open an IRA

An IRA is an individual retirement account that you can open at a bank or brokerage firm which consists of two types of IRAs: traditional and Roth. Traditional IRAs offer tax deductions on your contributions, while Roth IRAs offer tax-free withdrawals in retirement.

iii). Invest in stocks, bonds, and mutual funds

Stocks, bonds, and mutual funds are all types of investments that can help you grow your retirement savings over time.

iv). Begin saving on time

When you start saving for your retirement earlier, you will have more time to grow your money.

Maximizing Retirement Income

Maximizing retirement income is also a crucial aspect of retirement planning. It's important to work with a financial advisor to develop a personalized retirement income plan that meets individual needs and goals. There are several things you can do to maximize your retirement income. Some of the most important things include:

i). Ensure you understand your pension and Social Security benefits

You should know how much money you will receive from each source, and when you will start receiving benefits.

ii). Make sure you have enough saved for retirement

Let your investments grow over the years through compounding magic. The longer your money stays invested, the more it can multiply. An easy-to-use retirement calculator can show you how much you should save based on your current age, desired retirement age, and lifestyle goals. The use a retirement calculator to estimate how much money you will need.

iii). Work part-time after retirement

Retirement doesn't mean the end of fruitful endeavors. Embrace part-time work or freelancing after retiring. It not only brings in extra income but also keeps you engaged and fulfilled. This can help you supplement your retirement income.

iv). Downsize your home

Consider downsizing your home to release equity and improve your financial prospects. Smaller living means reduced expenses, like mortgage payments and utilities, leaving you with more financial flexibility. This can free up money that you can use for retirement.

v). Live on a budget

Budgeting plays a crucial role in achieving financial independence. Track your income and expenses, categorize costs, and find ways to adjust your spending to match your financial goals. This will help you make sure that your retirement income is enough to cover your expenses.

vi). Delaying Social Security benefits

Widows have the option to delay claiming Social Security benefits. By waiting until your full retirement age or beyond, which is 66 for most people,you can receive higher monthly benefits. Weigh the decision carefully, considering your health, life expectancy, and financial needs.For example, if a widow delays benefits until age 70, she will receive 132% of her full benefit amount.

vii). Annuities

Annuities are a type of insurance product that provides a guaranteed income stream for a set period of life. Annuities can be a good option for widows who want to ensure a steady stream of income in retirement.

Retirement planning is an important aspect of financial planning for widows. Understanding pensions and Social Security benefits, developing a strategy for saving for retirement, and maximizing retirement income are all crucial steps in achieving financial security in the later years. By taking a proactive approach and seeking guidance from trusted professionals, widows can achieve peace of mind and a secure financial future.

Chapter 6
Estate Planning for Widows

Estate planning is a critical component of widows' financial stability. It entails planning for the transfer of assets and property to heirs, minimizing taxes and expenses, and ensuring that one's final wishes are carried out. This chapter of the widow's financial manual focuses on three major components of estate preparation: comprehending wills and trusts, planning for incapacity, and reducing taxes and expenses.

Understanding wills and trusts is critical for widows who want their assets dispersed by their preferences. A will is a legal instrument that defines the distribution of an individual's assets shall be divided following their demise. In contrast, a trust is a legal framework that allows a third party or trustee to manage assets on behalf of the beneficiary. In contrast, a trust is a legal framework that allows a third party, or trustee, to administer assets on behalf of beneficiaries. Trusts can help to reduce taxes and expenses while also ensuring that assets are dispersed in a timely and effective manner.

Another key part of estate planning is planning for disability. This entails devising a strategy for handling one's affairs in the case of incapacity or infirmity. Appointing a power of attorney to make financial and healthcare decisions, making advance directives for end-of-life care, and establishing a living trust to manage assets in the case of incapacity are all examples of things you may do.

Finally, in estate planning, limiting taxes and expenses is critical. Techniques such as gifting assets during one's lifetime, forming trusts to hold assets, and leveraging tax-advantaged accounts may be used. Widows can maximize the value of their assets and guarantee that they are transferred according to their preferences by reducing taxes and expenses.

To summarize, estate planning is a vital component of widows' financial stability. Widows can guarantee that their assets are dispersed according to their preferences and that their financial future is safe by understanding wills and trusts, planning for incapacity, and avoiding taxes and expenses. Professional help from a financial advisor or estate planning attorney can be extremely beneficial in creating an effective estate plan.

Chapter 7

Debt Management

Losing a spouse brings an unimaginable emotional burden. Unfortunately, along with grief, death brings another problem, especially for the widows- the financial problems which may or may not last long depending on how it was handled. This can increase grief within the family.

In case your spouse who normally handles the financial aspect of your family dies and that led to you being late in paying up your bills, there are ways to reduce and clear your debt. Many of the surviving spouses have suffered great financial and personal hardship. This problem affects both men and women. Generally, it is assumed that women live longer than men as a result, widows unfairly face additional financial obligations.

Financial health requires getting professional help when you're in debt and understanding how your financial decisions affect Social Security. Most times, it is usually the widow who pays off any mortgage/debt through her income, valuables, or with the deceased life insurance. If you want to continue living in that same house, you may sell off the house and look for a smaller and more affordable apartment.

In case you possess an extensive understanding of various kinds of debt, it can assist you to develop suitable plans for managing outstanding liabilities. Debt can be classified as secured or unsecured. Collateral is like a human guarantor to the lender that he would get back his loan in one piece; so If you don't pay, they can get their money back. Secured debt has collateral, while unsecured debt has no collateral.

There exist multiple paths for widows to obtain financial aid.

For instance, programs like Social Security Survivor Benefits and Veterans Administration benefits offer monthly stipends to military widows to help them cover their living expenses. You can also receive the life insurance payments if your spouse had a policy. Many companies give survivor benefits, including pension plans and health insurance.

Additionally, there exist non-profits and charities that extend grants, and scholarships, alongside emergency funds geared towards assisting widows with unexpected fees similar to medical bills or home renovations.

It's crucial to recall that receiving monetary aid is not a lasting resolution. Widows should come up with a strong money plan that involves budgeting, handling debts, and saving for unexpected expenses. Obtaining professional advice can be advantageous in devising a personalized plan that considers your situation. Money management can be challenging for widows in financial distress.

Managing money involves creating budgets, keeping track of expenses, and setting financial goals. Talking to a financial or debt counselor can also provide support and guidance when dealing with debt. Knowing how financial choices can affect

Social Security payments, in the long run, is super important.

By navigating financial hardships and developing long-term strategies, widows can achieve financial security and independence. Widows need to gather information about their deceased spouse's life insurance, savings account balances, and previous employers' details including retirement accounts and company life insurance.

Seeking support from close family members is a viable option for financial help. If they explain the terms clearly, they might give loans with very low or no interest. This method stops disagreements and problems when dividing up belongings after the widow dies.

While there are government programs available to assist widows financially, they are not discussed in detail here. In addition to losing income, widows may face the task of handling any debts that were left by their deceased spouse. Must the surviving spouses pay these debts?

Usually, a spouse who is still alive doesn't have to take care of their partner's money owed after they pass away unless they both signed up for it together. This usually applies to loans related to a home, car, or credit card. If the loan does not include the name of the surviving spouse, they are not held accountable for repaying it. Still, in certain countries, both partners bear equal obligations for any debts they generate while being married.

Finding the best option for repaying your debts is very important for widows who want to secure the future of their finances. One approach is to prioritize paying off high-interest bills while making minimum payments on other loans. An alternative involves combining debts into one loan having a lower interest rate. This makes easier money transfers and lowers overall interest rates. To avoid future debt. It's important to budget, live within means, and avoid unnecessary expenses. Building a reserve for unexpected costs and steering clear of high-interest credit card debt is also key. Losing a spouse does not mean losing control over financial matters for women.

Chapter 8

Building an Emergency Fund

An emergency fund is a financial cushion that you can use to meet unforeseen expenses, such as a job loss, auto repair, or medical bill because life is full of unexpected occurrences and bills. It's crucial to maintain a contingency fund setup. This way, you can avoid depending on credit or loans when unexpected needs come. Building an emergency fund is a critical step in obtaining financial stability and peace of mind.

Understanding the aim of an emergency fund is the first step toward developing a strong financial foundation for yourself. An emergency fund acts as a necessary safety net, giving a financial buffer to meet unforeseen expenses that may develop suddenly. In this section, we will go more into the relevance of an emergency fund and how it can shield you from the traps of relying on high-interest loans or credit cards during times of crisis.

Protecting Against Unexpected Expenses

Life is full of uncertainty, and unexpected expenses might come at any moment. It might be a sudden medical emergency requiring rapid care, a significant car repair that must be postponed, or unanticipated home repairs. Without an emergency fund, individuals sometimes find themselves struggling to come up with funds, resorting to expensive borrowing options that can contribute to long-term financial stress.

Avoiding High-Interest Loans and Credit Cards

When faced with unforeseen bills, many people resort to credit cards or loans as a quick answer. Nonetheless, these solutions generally come with elevated interest rates. This can lead to a recurring sequence of financial obligations and fiscal strain. Having funds mapped out for emergencies will make you avoid taking high-interest loans thereby enabling you to take control over your financial situation.

Preserving Financial Security

An emergency fund provides a sense of financial security, delivering peace of mind during hard times. Knowing that you have a specific fund to manage unforeseen expenses allows you to maneuver through challenging situations without compromising your overall financial well-being. It decreases tension and anxiety, letting you focus on resolving the issue at hand rather than stressing about how to finance it.

Establishing Financial Resilience

Emergency funds are very important if you want to build strong financial resilience.

It enables you to weather unanticipated storms without derailing your long-term financial goals. By depending on your savings rather than external sources of credit, you maintain control over your money and avoid getting stuck in a cycle of debt.

Tailoring the Fund to Your Needs

The size of your emergency fund depends on numerous things, including your income, expenses, and unique circumstances. While the overall advice is to save three to six months' worth of living expenses, you can alter this to meet your unique situation. Factors such as work stability, health concerns, and family responsibilities may require a larger or smaller emergency fund. Assessing your needs and structuring a fund tailored to your situation ensures you are appropriately prepared for unanticipated events.

Recognizing the necessity of an emergency fund is a crucial component of financial planning. It acts as an essential instrument to defend against unforeseen expenses, avoid high-interest loans, and maintain financial stability.

By knowing the objective of an emergency fund, you can appreciate its value in providing a financial buffer during hard times. As you move forward in your financial path, prioritize developing an emergency fund to ensure your financial well-being and enjoy better peace of mind.

Setting Savings Goals and Creating a Dedicated Emergency Fund

The first step in developing an emergency fund is to set a savings target. The quantity of money you need in your contingency reserve will rely on your conditions.

When you are done calculating how much money you wanna save, start setting it aside every month. You can achieve this in many steps:

i). Assess Expenses

You can determine how much expenses you generate by computing your monthly average expenses. This includes housing, utilities, commute, provisions, medical care, financial obligations, and additional essential expenses.

You aim to save three to six months' worth of expenses as a general rule. However, evaluate your circumstances, such as work stability, dependents, and individual risk tolerance, to establish the proper size of your emergency fund.

ii). Set Realistic Goals

You don't have to try to play macho by saving too much money all at once. Divide your intended emergency fund amount into smaller reasonable goals for yourself and progressively raise your contributions each month to make it more practical and less daunting. You may determine how much you need to save each month to attain your emergency fund target within a set timeframe.

iii). Prioritize Saving

Just like you would with any other bill, make saving money a priority. This involves putting money aside for your emergency fund before you spend money on other things. Treat your emergency fund savings as a financial priority.

iv). Automate Your Savings

Direct Deposit: This is a terrific way to make sure you're saving money regularly, even if you forget to do it manually. Set up automatic transfers from your paycheck to your emergency fund, providing a constant and disciplined approach to saving.

v). Separate Account: Keep your emergency savings in a separate account, preferably one with high-yield interest, to avoid tapping into it for non-emergency uses.

vi). Cut Expenses and Increase Income

If you're finding it so hard to save up some cash, how about initiating by reducing certain unnecessary expenditures?

expenses? This could mean eating out less, canceling needless subscriptions, or finding cheaper methods to get around and channeling those savings toward your emergency fund. Explore options to enhance your income, such as taking on a side job or freelancing, to expedite your emergency fund savings.

vii). Stay Disciplined and Resist Temptation

Don't touch your emergency savings until it's an emergency. Avoid spending your emergency fund for non-emergency purposes. This will help you maintain your cash growth so that it's there when you truly need it.

viii). Track your spending

This can help you identify areas where you may cut back on your outlays to accumulate more funds.

By re-evaluating your emergency fund frequently to consider fluctuations in expenditures, revenue, or personal conditions. Adjust your savings objectives as needed.

ix). Rebuild and Replenish:

If you have to utilize your emergency fund for an unforeseen expense, it's crucial to replenish it as soon as possible. This is because your emergency fund is your financial safety net. It's there to assist you meet unforeseen expenses so that you don't have to go into debt or sell your possessions. Begin by saving a little bit of extra money every month.

This will help you rebuild your fund more quickly.

It's crucial to be patient and consistent when rebuilding your emergency fund because it is a long-term commitment. It might seem so hard for you initially. Yet it will yield results over time. While it may take time to attain your target, the peace of mind and the financial security it brings are important. Start small, stay focused, and enjoy each step towards obtaining your emergency fund goal.

It's vital to maintain a contingency fund set up. This way, you can avoid depending on credit or loans when unexpected needs come. Nonetheless, these solutions generally come with elevated interest rates. This can lead to a recurring sequence of financial obligations and fiscal strain. However, these options generally come with elevated interest rates. This can lead to a recurring pattern of monetary liabilities and fiscal strain.

Establishing Financial Resilience

If you desire to establish strong financial resilience, having an emergency fund is very important. The quantity of money you need in your contingency reserve will rely on your conditions. You can determine how much expenses you generate by computing your monthly average expenses. This includes housing, utilities, commute, provisions, medical care, financial obligations, and additional essential expenses.

If you're finding it so hard to save up some cash, how about initiating by reducing certain unnecessary expenditures?
This can help you identify areas where you may cut back on your outlays to accumulate more funds. By re-evaluating your emergency fund frequently to consider fluctuations in expenditures, revenue, or personal conditions. It

might seem so hard for you initially. Yet it will yield results over time.

Chapter 9

Financial Tech Tools To Aid The Widowed

Budgeting, investing, and financial planning might sound stressful, but fear not! Modern technology brings solutions to the palm of your hand. Leap into this digital universe with us, and emerge as a financially-empowered individual.

Looking at budgeting tools, Mint and YNAB shine brightly. Remember, understanding your cash flow—the in and out of your money—is the cornerstone of sound budgeting. These apps spoon-feed this information to you in simple, digestible chunks. You'll see your spending categories at a glance. Are you splurging a bit too much on takeouts? These apps will let you know. Little by little, you'll tweak your spending habits until you find your comfortable balance.

Similarly, investing tools, such as Acorns and Robinhood, demystify the world of investing. Long gone are the days of needing deep pockets to dip your toes in the investment pool. With only a few pennies, you can weave your way into portfolios that suit your needs. These tools are like training wheels for beginners, helping you maintain your balance while you learn the ropes. But be mindful, the market is not always smooth-sailing; storms can roll in, so invest wisely.

Moreover, financial planning apps like Personal Capital and PocketGuard are like your financial life narrated in one place. These data visualisation tools make it easy to see your financial health in an instant. Debts, investments, retirement plans, savings—all are weaved into a cohesive picture. Simplifying complex data into an easy-to-understand form, you can clearly plot the points of your financial journey and map your way forward.

Chapter 10

Navigating Tax Intricacies as a Widow

During your journey as a widow, tax challenges might appear to be a tough beast to tame. Yet, once you pull back the curtain of complexity, you'll find these beasts are more like kittens. Understanding your new tax circumstances doesn't have to feel like a marathon; consider it more of a leisurely stroll.

Think of "Qualifying Widow(er)" tax status as your new financial friend. For two years following the loss of your spouse, if you have a dependent child, you may file your taxes similar to how you did before, as a married couple. This can gift you with tax perks, such as broader tax brackets and higher standard deductions.

Next, let's peek at Inheritance Tax. Here's an exciting fact: typically, spouses are exempt from this tax! But don't celebrate too soon; tax rules are like chameleons—they change colours depending on your location and your estate's value. Engaging a tax advisor is like having a map in this ever-changing terrain.

Finally, let's visit the land of retirement account alterations. Suppose your spouse left behind individual retirement accounts

(IRAs). In that case, the fine print in the tax manuscript is subject to change based on whether you were the chosen beneficiary. Treading carefully here ensures that your journey doesn't detour into unexpected tax burdens.

Let knowledge arm you, lighting up your route to financial stability, illuminating surprises, and lighting your way to peace of mind.

Conclusion

To sum up, money management can seem challenging for anyone.

However, with a positive attitude and resources, the spouses who are bereaved can make progress to protect their financial stability. By analyzing their present financial condition, creating a financial plan, checking insurance plans, and choosing low-risk investment opportunities, widows can guarantee a future that is financially secure and stable.

Moreover, spreading their investment holdings, keeping an eye on transaction costs, consistently evaluating and adjusting their investment holdings, and looking for pro advice on money matters are also vital strategies for their financial security.

Creating a rainy reserve is yet another vital aspect of budgeting and saving. A sudden money can assist you handle unforeseen expenses, like for example, auto restorations or hospital bills. This enables you to manage all these costs without counting on plastic money or lending. Try to set aside a minimum of a range of 3 to 6 months' expenses money in your safety net.

When talking about handling debt, it's crucial to think about setting high-interest high-interest rates as the initial step. Paying the smallest amount on your credit cards can result in constant debt and more charges that can be challenging to break free from. By concentrating on settling expensive debt, you can hold on to currency in the distant future. That can additionally assist boost your overall financial well-being.

By seeking expert assistance, making a financial plan, saving for unexpected expenses, putting debt repayment first, and prioritizing necessities, widows can manage their money. Using these methods, individuals can accomplish economic stability. Although it might be difficult to handle your finances after the loss of a loved one, by having the correct mindset and aids, you can create a path for a more promising future.

www.ingramcontent.com/pod-product-compliance
Lightning Source LLC
Chambersburg PA
CBHW062333290526
45794CB00005B/2020